WHEN **pets** ATTACK!

OSTRICHES ARE NOT PETS!

Gareth Stevens
Publishing

BY HEATHER MOORE NIVER

Dedication: For Dad (I never believed your story about the ostrich!) and Oscar, of course.

Please visit our website, www.garethstevens.com. For a free color catalog of all our high-quality books, call toll free 1-800-542-2595 or fax 1-877-542-2596.

Library of Congress Cataloging-in-Publication Data

Niver, Heather Moore.
Ostriches are not pets / by Heather Moore Niver.
 p. cm. — (When pets attack)
Includes index.
ISBN 978-1-4339-9284-1 (pbk)
ISBN 978-1-4339-9285-8 (6-pack)
ISBN 978-1-4339-9283-4 (library binding)
1.Ostriches — Juvenile literature. 2. Wild animals as pets — Juvenile literature. I. Niver, Heather Moore. II. Title.
QL696.S9 N58 2014
598.5'24—dc23

First Edition

Published in 2014 by
Gareth Stevens Publishing
111 East 14th Street, Suite 349
New York, NY 10003

Copyright © 2014 Gareth Stevens Publishing

Designer: Katelyn E. Reynolds
Editor: Therese Shea

Photo credits: Cover, pp. 1, 23, 29 iStockphoto/Thinkstock.com; cover, pp. 1–32 (home sweet home image) © iStockphoto.com/DNY59; cover, pp. 1–32 (background) Hemera/Thinkstock.com; cover, pp. 1–32 (blood splatter), pp. 3–32 (frame) iStockphoto/Thinkstock.com; p. 5 John Foxx/Stockbyte/Thinkstock.com; p. 6 De Agnostini Picture Library/Getty Images; p. 7 Kip Ross/National Geographic/Getty Images; p. 9 Hoberman Collection/UIG via Getty Images; p. 10 loflo69/Shutterstock.com; p. 11 Carolyn A. McKeone/ Photo Researchers/Getty Images; p. 12 Eric Isselee/Shutterstock.com; p. 13 Heinrich van den Berg/Gallo Images/Getty Images; p. 15 HPH Publishing/Getty Images; p. 17 Ondacaracola/Shutterstock.com; p. 18 Theo Allofs/Stone/Getty Images; pp. 20–21 Wild Horizons/UIG via Getty Images; p. 25 Steve & Ann Toon/ Robert Harding World Imagery/Getty Images; p. 27 swakopphoto.com/Shutterstock.com; p. 28 Dave King/ Dorling Kindersley/Getty Images.

Printed in the United States of America

CPSIA compliance information: Batch #CS13GS: For further information contact Gareth Stevens, New York, New York at 1-800-542-2595.

CONTENTS

THE ODD OSTRICH

An ostrich is a strange-looking bird. It has long legs and a large body covered with **shaggy** feathers. On top of its skinny neck is a small head with bulging eyes. This bird's funny shape almost makes it look like a cartoon!

Ostriches can't fly, but they're fast. Some reach speeds of 43 miles (70 km) per hour. And they can be dangerous, too. One powerful ostrich kick can kill! These are two reasons ostriches don't make good pets. Ostriches are wild animals, and they're best suited to their **habitats** or very large farms—not homes. Read on to learn more about this amazing bird.

ooooh... SHINY!

Ostriches like little objects that shine. If an ostrich sees a bright glittering object, the curious bird will try to peck at it. It's smart to avoid wearing anything that might shine in the sun, like buttons or snaps, if you're going to visit an ostrich!

Ostriches have been on Earth for more than 100 million years!

BIG BIRDS

Ostriches aren't just big—they're the biggest birds in the world. An adult ostrich may be 7 to 9 feet (2.1 to 2.7 m) tall, while the average human male is only about 5.6 feet (1.7 m) tall. Ostriches are heavy, too. They can weigh 220 to 350 pounds (100 to 160 kg).

An animal of this size can't live just anywhere. Ostriches are sometimes very unhappy in **captivity**. If they don't have enough space, they begin to act oddly. They might scream, pluck out their own or other ostriches' feathers, or even hurt themselves.

plenty of PREDATORS

The ostrich may be big, fast, and strong, but that doesn't stop other animals from trying to hunt it. Some of the ostrich's main predators include cheetahs, hyenas, crocodiles, and lions. These animals often hunt newly hatched ostrich chicks, too. People are another ostrich enemy!

An ostrich's size seems even more incredible when you see one next to a person.

WHAT A WOBBLE!

Ostriches like wide-open spaces so they can run and stretch their long legs. They don't like areas thick with trees or lots of bushes. Most ostriches are found in the **savannas** and deserts of Africa.

Ostriches are happiest living together in groups. These groups are called herds, troops, or wobbles! Most of the time, a wobble is made up of about 10 birds, but it can have as many as 100 ostriches. That's an awful lot of big, fast birds in one place! Most people don't have enough land to keep one or more ostriches happy.

kinds of OSTRICHES

There are four kinds, or species, of ostriches today. The Southern ostrich (or South African ostrich) is found in southern Africa. The North African ostrich (or red-necked ostrich) lives in parts of western and eastern Africa. The Masai ostrich and the Somali ostrich are found only in eastern Africa.

Sometimes, an ostrich wobble may adopt the young from another herd.

Ostrich eggs aren't well hidden, so they need to be protected day and night.

10

nesting DOWN LOW

Each ostrich wobble has a **dominant** male and female. The dominant, or alpha, male is usually in charge of the wobble. After mating, the female ostriches, or hens, put their eggs in one nest. The dominant hen puts hers in the middle of the nest where they're safest. Ostrich eggs are white or yellowish. Even though the eggs are mixed, each mother can tell which are hers!

Mom and dad ostriches take turns sitting on the eggs to protect them and keep them warm. The alpha male sits on them at night, and the dominant female takes the day shift.

A flightless bird as big as an ostrich can't build a nest up in a tree like a lot of birds do. Instead, the male digs a shallow hole in the ground for the "clutch" of eggs. The clutch **incubates** for about 45 days.

11

EGGS-CEPTIONAL EGGS

Unsurprisingly, ostriches lay the largest eggs of all birds. One ostrich egg weighs about 3 pounds (1.4 kg). A female ostrich can lay up to 100 eggs in one season, but usually lays 20 to 40. Either way, that's a lot of new ostriches to take care of! However, because ostrich nests are on the ground, predators such as hyenas sometimes eat eggs. People eat ostrich eggs, too.

Ostrich chicks that survive grow quickly—about 10 inches (25 cm) each month for the first 6 months. They can be 7 feet (2.1 m) tall just 18 months after they're born!

chick CARE

Ostrich chicks are cute, but they're a lot of work. In captivity, young chicks need an enclosed, movable pen that's at least 12 feet (3.7 m) long. They must be in a heated area each night. Chicks need lots of exercise, too. Without enough space to run, their legs won't grow correctly.

A hyena eats an ostrich egg in southern Africa.

PLEASE PASS THE SAND?

Ostriches are omnivores, which means they eat almost anything that's available. They don't have teeth, though. They eat small stones and sand, which help them break down food in their **gizzard**. Ostriches don't swallow their food right away. As an ostrich eats, food collects at the top of its throat in a space called the "crop." When the lump of food gets heavy enough, it slides down its neck.

Ostrich intestines are 46 feet (14 m) long! That's twice as long as a person's. Superlong intestines help an ostrich get lots of **nutrients** from its food.

leaves, locusts, AND LIZARDS

Ostriches are always trying to find something tasty. Usually, they eat plants, roots, leaves, and seeds. Sometimes they snack on insects such as **locusts** and small animals such as lizards. In captivity, ostriches have been known to eat just about anything they can swallow—including coins and clocks!

Ostriches get water from the plants they eat. However, they drink when they're near a water source.

FAST AND FEATHERED

Ostrich feet have a special shape. Ostriches are the only bird with just two toes on each foot. Their feet don't just hold up their heavy bodies. They help them get around extremely fast.

Ostriches are the fastest two-footed, or bipedal, animals on the planet. They can run up to 43 miles (70 km) an hour for about 20 minutes. They can run about 30 miles (48 km) an hour for longer periods. An ostrich's legs are so long that the space between its steps can be as wide as 16 feet (4.9 m). You wouldn't want to chase an escaped ostrich!

two TOES

Ostrich feet, with their two toes, act like hooves. They're built for running. The bottoms of the feet are padded and tough. The inside toes can be as long as 7 inches (18 cm). Unlike a hoof, each of these toes has a long, sharp claw, called a talon.

Most birds have three or four toes on each foot, but the ostrich only needs two.

Some ostrich "jockeys" don't use reins or a saddle.

They hold on to the wings to stay on the big bird.

Even ostriches raised by people sometimes attack. They kick with a powerful slashing motion made more deadly by the long talon on each foot. Ostriches have also been known to chase people and dogs. Both male and female ostriches can even kill lions!

In ancient Egypt, ostriches were used to pull chariots, two-wheeled carts for racing or war. Sometimes people rode ostriches, too. This practice didn't last very long, though, because many ostriches have bad tempers. Not many people want to ride an animal likely to kick or attack them.

Ostriches are still raced in certain places, such as South Africa. Riders place saddles on the ostriches and direct them with reins, just like in horse racing. However, ostriches are harder to ride than horses. Ostrich races, though unusual, have been held in some US cities, too.

Land-Animal Speed Records

ANIMAL	SPEED
cheetah	70 miles (113 km) per hour
ostrich	43 miles (70 km) per hour
person	27 miles (43 km) per hour

WHY WINGS?

If ostriches are runners and not fliers, why do they have wings? Their small wings aren't completely useless. Ostrich wings are like **rudders** that help them steer and change direction as they run. Wings also help ostriches keep warm or cool off. In addition, each wing has two "fingers" with sharp claws that can be used to fight enemies.

Ostriches often flirt with their wings. Male ostriches hold their heads up and fluff their feathers to scare off other males and attract a mate. They stomp and spread out their wings to look bigger.

birds of a different FEATHER

Ostriches have soft, loose feathers that look bushy because they don't hook together as other birds' feathers do. Most birds have a special **gland** that helps protect their feathers from water. Ostriches don't have this gland, so their feathers get wet in the rain.

Male ostriches have black feathers on their body with white feathers on their wings and tail. Females are brownish gray.

NOT VERY BRAINY

An ostrich has very large eyes. In fact, the ostrich has the largest eyes of any animal living on land! Each ostrich eye is about 2 inches (5 cm) across. That's almost the same size as the balls used to play pool.

Ostrich eyes take up most of the space in their head, so there isn't much room for a brain. An ostrich's brain is actually smaller than one of its eyeballs! These big birds aren't very brainy. When they're scared, they sometimes run in circles—not the smartest way to get away from a predator!

not that DUMB

Many people think ostriches bury their head in the ground when they're frightened. That's a tall tale. Ostriches hide—and sleep—with their long neck stretched flat against the ground. The color of their head and neck helps them blend in with the ground. However, from far away, it looks like their head is buried.

Its big eyes allow an ostrich to see far across its savanna or desert habitat.

SAVED BY THE BELT?

Ostriches are increasingly kept as livestock, but that still doesn't make them good pets. When they're scared or threatened, they jump around, flap their wings, and can easily knock someone over. And we know their kick can hurt—or even kill—someone. Owners have to be very careful at all times.

Famous country musician Johnny Cash had several ostriches on his ranch in Tennessee. One harsh winter, some of his ostriches died. One ostrich was upset over losing his mate and kicked Cash, breaking several of the singer's ribs. Luckily, Cash was wearing a huge belt buckle, which protected him from even worse injuries.

wanted: OSTRICHES

Ostriches aren't in danger of becoming **extinct**, but they've been hunted or used as livestock for years. Their feathers are used to decorate clothes and clean machinery. Their strong skin is used to make shoes, bags, and coats. Some people eat ostrich meat because it's healthier than other meats.

Ostriches kick about twice as hard as a professional boxer can punch!

THE CAMEL BIRD

The scientific name for the ostrich is *Struthio camelus*. In ancient times, people called the ostrich the "camel bird" because both ostriches and camels can go a long time without drinking water. That's why they can live in deserts.

Most birds like to take dust baths. This means they roll around in the sand to dry their feathers and shake off bugs. Ostriches like to do this, too. Can you imagine such a big bird making that much dust in your yard? It would be a big mess! Ostriches like to take baths in water, too.

long-distance CALL

Ostriches normally don't make much noise. However, when they do make sounds—they're loud! Their calls can be heard from long distances. Ostrich noises include whistles, growls, hisses, and even roars. Males make the most sounds to warn off other males during mating time.

It seems strange to think a dust bath could clean a bird. However, all the moving around can shake off tiny, harmful creatures.

ALL IN THE FAMILY

Ostriches are related to animals that don't exist anymore: dinosaurs! All birds are related to dinosaurs, actually. However, studying ostriches in particular is helping scientists understand how bipedal dinosaurs such as the *Tyrannosaurus rex* may have walked around.

Plenty of ostriches still roam Earth, but the Arabian ostrich, also called the Middle Eastern ostrich, has been extinct since 1966. Organizations keep an eye on ostrich populations so other kinds don't disappear, too. They may not make ideal pets, but we still want these birds around for as long as possible!

got a license for THAT OSTRICH?

It's legal in many places to keep ostriches, but many states require owners to have special permits. Because ostriches require special care, owners can expect officials to check that the birds are in good health and in safe, clean conditions.

kiwi

Ostriches: Extreme Birds

BIGGEST BIRD	9 feet (2.7 m) tall
LARGEST EGGS	5.5 inches x 7 inches (14 cm x 18 cm)
HEAVIEST EGGS	3 pounds (1.4 kg)
FASTEST ON LAND	43 miles (70 km) per hour
BIGGEST EYES	2 inches (5 cm) across

Ostriches are part of the oldest group of birds, called ratites, which includes the emus of Australia and the kiwis of New Zealand.

emu

GLOSSARY

captivity: the state of being caged

dominant: most important or strongest

extinct: no longer living

gizzard: part of the stomach of birds where food is broken down by muscles

gland: a body part that produces something needed for a bodily function

habitat: the natural place where an animal or plant lives

incubate: to keep eggs warm so they can hatch

locust: a bug similar to a grasshopper

nutrient: something a living thing needs to grow and stay alive

rudder: something used like the part on a boat or plane that helps steer

savanna: a grassland with scattered patches of trees

shaggy: growing long and uneven

FOR MORE INFORMATION

Books

Stout, Frankie. *Ostriches: Nature's Biggest Birds*. New York, NY: PowerKids Press, 2009.

White, Mel. *National Geographic Angry Birds: 50 True Stories of the Fed Up, Feathered, and Furious*. Washington, DC: National Geographic, 2012.

Websites

Ostrich
animal.discovery.com/animals/life/ostrich.html
Find out more interesting information about ostriches.

Ostrich (*Struthio camelus*)
www.arkive.org/ostrich/struthio-camelus/#src=portletV3api
Learn fun facts about these big flightless birds.

Ostriches
kids.nationalgeographic.com/kids/animals/creaturefeature/ostrich/
Photos, maps, and videos tell us more about the wild ostrich.

INDEX